S0-CPF-489

At the Art Museum

By Melissa Hogendorp

Illlustrated by Ron Lieser

"Hurry, Caitlin, we're going to miss the bus."
My sister, Jeanne, is always rushing me. She thinks
if we're not waiting for the bus for fifteen minutes,
we're late. But even I didn't plan to be late today.
The fifth graders are going on a field trip to the
Art Institute. I think it's the best place ever.

I want to be an artist. I'm taking art classes
and am learning how to use light and shadow in
my art.

Last week, my teacher displayed my charcoal drawing on the wall in our classroom. I hope my paintings are hung in art galleries someday.

"Caitlin, don't forget your sketchbook!" Jeanne exclaimed.

I nodded and quickly packed my sketchbook in my backpack so I could sketch some of the paintings at the Art Institute.

When the bus finally arrived, I grabbed a window seat and waited for Jason, my best friend.

Jason is an artist too, but he likes to draw irregular shapes. Sometimes his lines are so blurred they look almost invisible. I like crisp, bold lines. My pictures of dogs look like dogs, but Jason's don't.

At the Art Institute, the classes divided into small groups. Jason and I were in the same group. He wanted to head to the modern art hall first, but I wanted to observe the exhibit of United States art.

"Don't worry. We'll see both exhibits before the day is over," our leader noted.

First, we went to see paintings from the United States. I headed straight for the painting by Grant Wood. For some reason, this painting is just irresistible to me. It shows a woman and man standing in front of their farmhouse. He's wearing overalls, a jacket, and is holding a pitchfork. She's wearing a plain dress with a stiff white collar.

I called Jason to come check out the Grant
Wood painting I wanted to sketch.

"Hey, Jason, isn't this an impressive pai. . . ?"
Before I knew it, the painting was gone! I thought
to myself, was it stolen? No, that's impossible! The
security guards in the museum would notice the
theft right away.

"Maybe it's being cleaned," suggested Jason.
That didn't seem likely, but I was determined to
find out what had happened to it.

Jason looked around the hall and found someone to ask. "Where's the Grant Wood painting?" he inquired. "It's missing."

She chuckled. "Well, yes, it's missing, but it isn't lost. It's being relocated to another part of the museum. You can view it next Sunday."

Needless to say, I was relieved that the painting was not stolen, but what would I sketch instead? Jason took me to a red, white, blue, and black painting.

"Look," he said, "isn't this incredible?" I had
to admit it was. It had things Jason and I both
like in art. The artist had signed his painting, but
I couldn't read his writing because it was illegible.
We decided to sketch it, but we didn't have time to
finish.

All too soon, we were back on the bus and
on our way home. This was definitely the most
exciting field trip ever!